BACKYARD WILDLIFE
Mice

by Kari Schuetz

BLASTOFF! READERS

BELLWETHER MEDIA • MINNEAPOLIS, MN

Note to Librarians, Teachers, and Parents:

Blastoff! Readers are carefully developed by literacy experts and combine standards-based content with developmentally appropriate text.

Level 1 provides the most support through repetition of high-frequency words, light text, predictable sentence patterns, and strong visual support.

Level 2 offers early readers a bit more challenge through varied simple sentences, increased text load, and less repetition of high-frequency words.

Level 3 advances early-fluent readers toward fluency through increased text and concept load, less reliance on visuals, longer sentences, and more literary language.

Level 4 builds reading stamina by providing more text per page, increased use of punctuation, greater variation in sentence patterns, and increasingly challenging vocabulary.

Level 5 encourages children to move from "learning to read" to "reading to learn" by providing even more text, varied writing styles, and less familiar topics.

Whichever book is right for your reader, Blastoff! Readers are the perfect books to build confidence and encourage a love of reading that will last a lifetime!

This edition first published in 2014 by Bellwether Media, Inc.

No part of this publication may be reproduced in whole or in part without written permission of the publisher. For information regarding permission, write to Bellwether Media, Inc., Attention: Permissions Department, 5357 Penn Avenue South, Minneapolis, MN 55419.

Library of Congress Cataloging-in-Publication Data

Schuetz, Kari, author.
  Mice / by Kari Schuetz.
     pages cm. – (Blastoff! Readers. Backyard Wildlife)
  Summary: "Developed by literacy experts for students in kindergarten through grade three, this book introduces mice to young readers through leveled text and related photos"– Provided by publisher.
  Audience: Ages 5-8.
  Audience: K to grade 3.
  Includes bibliographical references and index.
  ISBN 978-1-62617-060-5 (hardcover : alk. paper)
  1. Mice–Juvenile literature. 2. Muridae–Juvenile literature. I. Title. II. Series: Blastoff! readers. 1, Backyard wildlife.
  QL737.R6S38 2014
  599.35'3–dc23
                         2013037390

Printed in the United States of America, North Mankato, MN.

Contents

What Are Mice?   4

Nests   8

Eating   12

Predators   18

Glossary   22

To Learn More   23

Index   24

Mice are small **rodents**. They have long, hairless tails.

Mice **scurry** around forests and grasslands. Some even live in **deserts**.

Mice build
nests in trees,
burrows, and
between rocks.

They care for babies inside their nests. They also store food there.

Mice **forage** for food at night. They search for fruits, seeds, and **insects**.

Mice stand on their back feet to eat. They grip food with their front feet.

They **gnaw**
on their food.
They need to
wear down
their long teeth.

Mice must look out for danger. Foxes, snakes, and **raptors** hunt them for dinner.

Mice can run forward or backward to escape these **predators**. To the nest, mouse!

Glossary

burrows—holes in the ground that some animals dig

deserts—dry lands with little rain

forage—to go out in search of food

gnaw—to bite or nibble on something for a long time

insects—small animals with six legs and hard outer bodies; insect bodies are divided into three parts.

predators—animals that hunt other animals for food

raptors—birds that have sharp vision, strong claws, and curved beaks; raptors hunt and eat other animals for food.

rodents—small animals with front teeth that grow throughout life

scurry—to run around in a hurry

To Learn More

AT THE LIBRARY

Donaldson, Julia. *The Gruffalo*. New York, N.Y.: Dial Books for Young Readers, 1999.

Numeroff, Laura. *If You Give a Mouse a Cookie*. New York, N.Y.: Laura Geringer Books, 2007.

Tait, Leia. *Mice*. New York, N.Y.: Weigl, 2010.

ON THE WEB

Learning more about mice is as easy as 1, 2, 3.

1. Go to www.factsurfer.com.

2. Enter "mice" into the search box.

3. Click the "Surf" button and you will see a list of related Web sites.

With factsurfer.com, finding more information is just a click away.

Index

babies, 10
burrows, 8
danger, 18
deserts, 6
eat, 14
escape, 20
feet, 14
food, 10, 12, 14, 16
forage, 12
forests, 6
foxes, 18
fruits, 12
gnaw, 16
grasslands, 6
insects, 12

nests, 8, 10, 20
night, 12
predators, 20
raptors, 18
rodents, 4
scurry, 6
seeds, 12
snakes, 18
tails, 4
teeth, 16
trees, 8

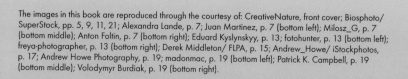